The ELEGANCE and COMFORT of HOME

DANA WOLTER
with CLINTON SMITH

Gibbs Smith

For Ann, Ellie, and Lucy

and for my husband, Danny

INTRODUCTION

AS AN INTERIOR DESIGNER, my goal has always been to create spaces that are not just visually beautiful but, more importantly, functional and livable for the entire family. I believe that the places in which we live should reflect who we are while also providing comfort and support to our overall well-being. I learned the importance of this firsthand when diagnosed in 2022 with stage 4 non-Hodgkin lymphoma. For the four months of my treatment, I was pretty much confined to my home for three out of four weeks each month. My home became my refuge, and it was a wonderful reminder of how important my surroundings were for me to heal and rest.

Aside from my faith, my family is most important to me, and they are at the heart of everything I do. I see a home as a sanctuary, a place where families—however small or large—can come together, recharge, and create memories that last a lifetime.

Whether it's a warm, inviting kitchen where everyone gathers or a cozy living room for afternoon naps, I want the design to look not only gracious but also support the family's daily life in a meaningful way, down to every little beautiful ritual—or mundane

task! I love using timeless furnishings and classic design elements that instill a sense of permanence and longevity. While trends come and go, these pieces ensure that the home remains functional and elegant for years to come.

My design process always starts with understanding how the family lives in their space and what we can do to help them live better. I think about how they move through the home, where they spend the most time, and what we can add to a room that pulls them in. We also try to look ahead at how the home can evolve as a family grows and needs change over time.

I enjoy getting to know my clients and spending time with them on a personal level to learn about their lifestyle, preferences, what they value, and what makes them, again, truly feel at home. Each family is different, and I want to create spaces that reflect their own unique stories, not someone else's ideal. I find it wildly rewarding to weave personal details into my designs, constructing spaces that are not just welcoming, but also meaningful. By really understanding each family's needs, I can then create homes that feel authentic and nurturing, ones they will love living in every day and that support them through life's ups and downs.

When it comes to beauty, I've always felt a home should do more than just please the eye: it should create a sense of peace and well-being. I strive for a balance between sophistication and comfort, using clean lines, soft textures, and neutral palettes to evoke calm and serenity. While I love incorporating luxurious materials and custom details, my goal is to never overwhelm the space. Instead, I aim for an understated elegance that is collected and approachable. My clients should feel as if they want to linger in their home and take pleasure in it, not just admire it from afar.

I have always been drawn to natural materials like wood, stone, and organic fabrics because they look better with age and with a little patina. Since my cancer diagnosis, I have become even more aware of using these materials and connecting the home to nature. I love bringing elements of the outdoors in—whether through natural light or outdoor views—because I believe that connection to nature is essential for well-being. A space that is easy to maintain, more beautiful with wear, and thoughtfully designed—all while being eminently practical—supports a more peaceful way of living.

As many clients have become personal friends over the past twenty years, my work goes beyond creating stylish interiors. Each project is extremely personal to me, and there is nothing more rewarding than watching a house transform into a home that works well for everyday life. Through my designs, some of which are showcased in this book, I hope to help families create homes that are not only truly their own but also places where they can find solace and thrive.

INTERPLAY *of* LIGHT *and* DARK

Interpreting the clients' needs and desires is one of our favorite parts of the job. Sometimes, they come to initial meetings with piles of inspiration or links to online mood boards. Other times, the directive is more succinct, as it was with the clients who hired us to design and decorate this French-inflected house in Mountain Brook, Alabama. As we began the renovation, the wife shared a few images, and we immediately embraced the palette of rich greens, rust, and sumptuous browns that she favored. Luckily for us, our firm loves to create using this palette.

The interplay between dark and light inspires us, especially when getting the mix of furnishings and fabrics just right. When we incorporated color into the fabric of this house, we used it selectively and judiciously to balance the unifying neutrals. With the exception of a few select patterned prints, primarily solid hues grace key areas: the pops of saturated color on pillows and window treatments really attract the eye and create a sense of overall harmony, while patterned fabrics in these same spaces might have proved overly distracting.

We also incorporated a number of dark wood furnishings—a blend of new pieces and choice antiques—to give the rooms a bit of "weight," so to speak. They anchor the spaces, giving the feeling of the rooms having been created over time. In a subtle way, they add a sense of permanence and longevity.

As in all of our firm's projects, creating comfort was important here. The dining room, for example, features plush upholstered chairs on casters that encourage guests to linger. To keep the room from being visually cluttered, skirted chairs hide multiple chair legs vying for attention next to the antique table, which is a standout piece. The chairs have a graceful curvature, but they are also quiet in their demeanor—not every piece of furniture in a room has to be the star of the show—and it's important to know where you want to focus the attention. Is it a piece of furniture, artwork, or perhaps a fabulous chandelier?

Another important aspect of this house was the clients' willingness to commit to such quality, time-honored materials as the exquisite wood cabinetry, millwork, and beautiful stone slabs that are present throughout the home. These are featured in both public and private spaces, from the kitchen to powder room to bedrooms. That dedication to materials creates a timeless sensibility. This is an inheritable house, one that's worthy of being passed down from one generation to the next.

White oak paneling
complements the room's
soft furnishings, creating a
welcoming space to gather.

A spacious custom banquette in the breakfast area
can accommodate an intimate or larger group.

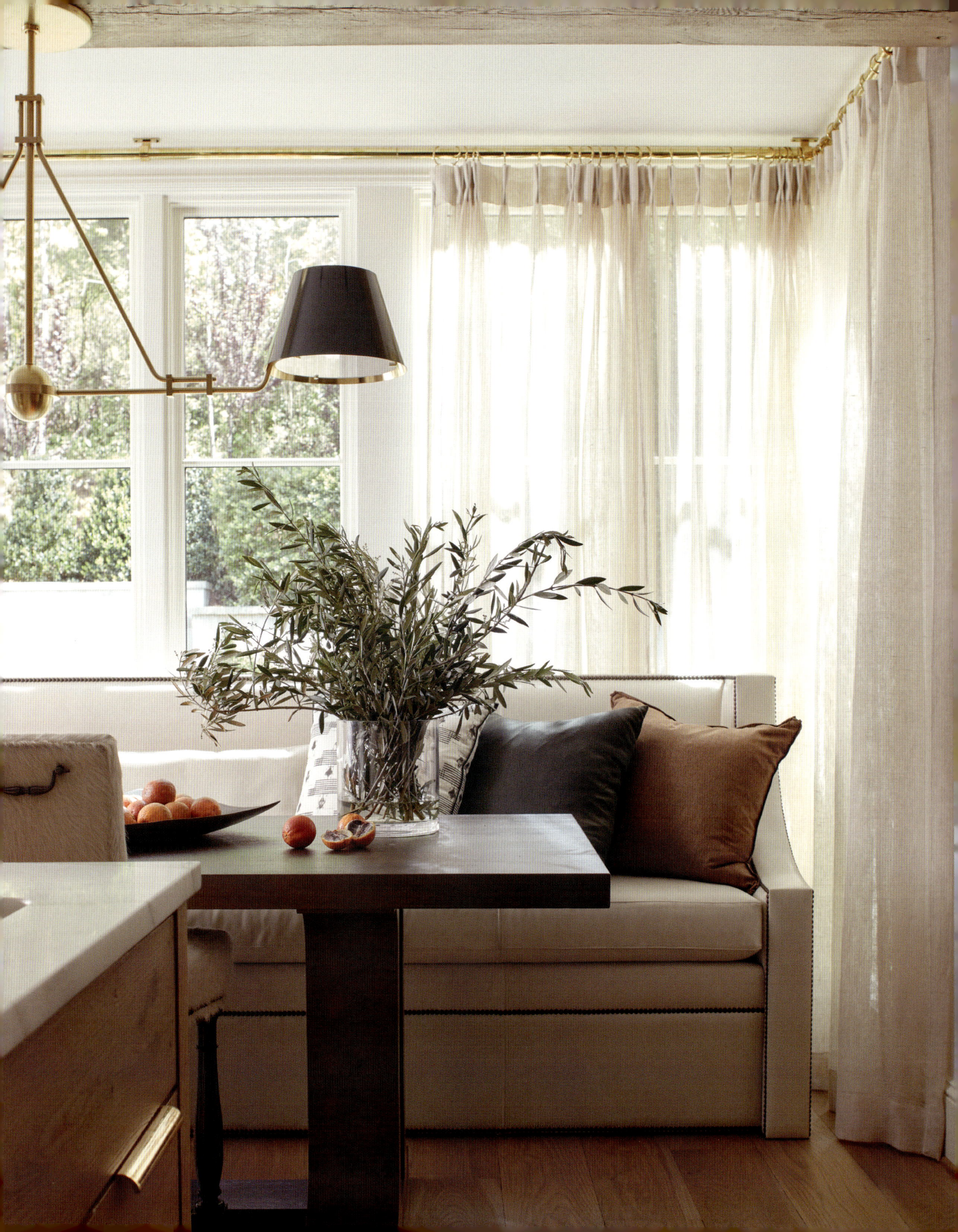

Candlesticks add visual repetition and rhythm to the dining room, both with their stately silhouettes and varying heights.

In a twist on open-concept living, the kitchen wall features a glass partition and window that open up to the family room when desired.

One of the kitchen's two islands allows for meal preparation, while the other has seating for dining. Two graceful lanterns help anchor the room, highlighting other brass accents.

TERRY O'NEILL

EERO SAARINEN: FURNITURE

When entertaining, an antique table in the living room is ideal for a makeshift bar.

A sisal carpet with a thick weave grounds the family room, incorporating additional texture in a subtle way. The natural material also adds an organic feel to the space.

*It can be the subtle details—not just
on the exterior, but on the interior—that
give a home a feeling of permanence.*

The powder room vanity echoes the design of the kitchen cabinetry, while an antique mirror allows for a special moment in the dramatic space. Another bathroom, opposite, features a marble-clad walk-in shower.

In this guest bedroom, we designed a custom headboard that extends along one entire wall. In the guest bathroom, opposite, small marble slabs are used as wainscoting, a nice contrast to the room's herringbone flooring design.

Placed to maximize outdoor views
from the living room, the desk
area is ideal for working or repose.

The home's traditional facade belies the mix of
classic and contemporary furnishings found within.

HISTORIC CHARM
in a NEW HOME

Sometimes a great house can emerge from extraordinary and challenging circumstances. That was certainly the case for our clients in Huntsville, Alabama, whose previous residence was destroyed in a devastating fire. Yet their determination to build anew in their beloved historic neighborhood led to the creation of this special home that embodies their grace and generosity. With newly constructed houses, it can be the subtle details—not just on the exterior, but on the interior—that give a home a feeling of permanence. It was important for us, together with the client and architect, to create new rooms that embodied the same charm as the historic homes scattered throughout the area.

An airy palette of soft grays, blues, and creams envelops the house, creating a sense of serenity that carries from one room to the next. Subtly stained hardwood floors and waxed finishes on the custom cabinetry add a sense of seamless continuity to the rooms. In a world of countless options, it takes real discipline and restraint to adhere to a finely restrained palette as we did here, but the results led to beautiful spaces that are far more than the sum of their individual parts.

Our firm undertakes a range of work and design styles. This clients' house leans toward the more traditional, and we kept the design spacious and classic without feeling overly formal or stodgy. We devoted a great deal of energy to the interior architecture, with its soaring twelve-foot-tall ceilings throughout most of the rooms, specifying custom built-ins, wall niches, and unique molding. These details helped ground the rooms and added texture to the large expanses of restrained surfaces.

When decorating rooms with such high ceilings and open space, there can be a tendency to overfurnish, an eagerness to "fill the space" simply because it is there. Here, we took a counterintuitive approach, going for scale rather than quantity of objects. There are no dainty furnishings here. Many of the pieces have detailed, sculptural lines that support an almost architectural feeling. Large-scaled upholstered pieces add a softness to the vast rooms, and floor-to-ceiling diaphanous window treatments gently filter the sunlight.

With so much light and the strong sense of airiness that permeates the home, we chose to go bold and dark in a handful of more intimate spaces. One is the butler's pantry, for which we selected rich navy walls. Another is a passageway that's punctuated with a dramatic metallic wall covering on the ceiling. It's really fun—and often surprising—to do something a little more daring in these sometimes overlooked, pass-through spaces. Details like these offer pleasing and even amusing little punctuation marks in a sea of tranquility.

Upon entry, guests are immediately greeted by this majestic sculptural staircase in the foyer. An adjacent hallway, opposite, highlights an upholstered wall for added texture and dimension.

A passageway offers a stylish vignette. Leaning art against a mirror or larger piece of art gives a casual flair.

The powder room, opposite, features a sculptural stone sink, which adds patina and a sense of antiquity.

The wallpaper in the dining room is by Phillip Jeffries. The blossoms on the trees evoke spring year-round.

The living room's beautiful
beams add a sense of
warmth and patina.

Bookcases and a paneling-clad niche were added to bring extra depth to the room, as well as a sense of intimacy with the newly created seating area.

Sometimes a great house can emerge from extraordinary and challenging circumstances.

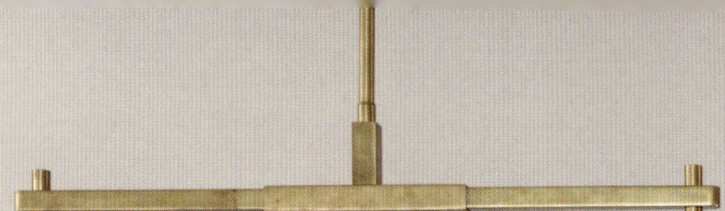

The kitchen's dining area is a favorite place to gather. The corner sink is an unexpected touch.

Our firm designed the cabinetry for the kitchen. We love the simple lines of the plaster range hood.

With its dark paint color and striking marble countertops and backsplash, the butler's pantry is a departure from the rest of the light-filled house. It's a welcome surprise to all who encounter it.

We designed a sculptural niche
that allowed us to upholster
the back of the bed wall for
added interest. A room entirely
wrapped in the pattern could
have been overwhelming but
using pattern judiciously makes it
all the more special.

The primary bedroom's color palette is an excellent example of melding the home's lighter and darker hues. The room's white walls are perfectly juxtaposed with the accent wall and dark headboard. The primary bathroom's tub, opposite, is "framed" by a wall of marble behind it, making it a sculptural—and inviting—centerpiece of the space.

We created a soothing guest bedroom by accenting the space with crisp periwinkle accents.

In the wife's office, a horizontal stripe wallpaper makes the room feel larger than it actually is. A built-in desk and storage offer plenty of space to work in a clutter-free environment.

A bathroom connected to the husband's office features white oak cabinets in a custom finish. We designed the vanity and chose blackened steel hardware for the drawers.

A verdant pattern on the laundry room's roman shades makes household chores and tasks feel more cheerful.

COMFORT AWAY
from HOME

H

ow you live in a primary residence isn't necessarily what you want or need in a vacation home, and we are often presented with that scenario in our design work with clients who have multiple residences. When it came to designing a destination home for Alabama-based clients who were building in central Florida, flexibility was key.

We showed the clients two different options for the living room layout, and they chose the open-concept floor plan. While this type of plan with the kitchen on full display can create challenges, it also offers the benefits of open and shared spaces. We focused the attention of the seating configuration on views of the outdoors and toward the TV and entertainment area. In this way, family members and friends are still very much connected to what's happening in the kitchen, without it being the primary focus.

We were fortunate to be brought onboard while the house was under construction and were therefore able to specify quite a number of custom furniture pieces to fit the rooms. This might sound intimidating, but creating something custom can often maximize a room to its fullest potential.

When it came to the color palette, we focused on muted jewel tones for accents—subdued purples, soft blues, maroons, and navy.

As for the home's pièce de résistance, it is the eye-popping dining room with its velvet-clad walls in the most indulgent shade of gray-blue. Located directly off the foyer, it immediately sets the tone upon entering the home, suggesting so much more to be discovered as one wanders throughout. The home's mix of furnishings and colors allows it to suit a variety of needs, whether for work or play for these clients.

With variations on purple, blue, maroon, and navy, the home's crisp palette is evident upon entry.

The living room celebrates the juxtaposition of dark and light accents.

Comfortable English-style chairs and a complementary wood table anchor the dining room, which was tricky to design because the space opens into other rooms on three sides and serves as sort of a passageway.

One main wall provides a
focal point in the dining room,
adorned by contemporary art
and an antique buffet. The space
is enveloped in a rich blue velvet,
which is dramatic both during
the day and at night, when
illuminated by candlelight.

Nailhead-clad doors conceal storage, while the diamond design adds additional architectural interest to the room.

In rooms with multiple functions,
we choose lighting that blends
and doesn't necessarily match.

Designed for a large family, the
leather banquette, opposite,
lends itself well to beachside
vacation living.

Most kitchen islands are simple rectangles. This one sports a decorative curved marble countertop as well as sculptural legs. The arched shape of the counter stools echoes that of the pendants.

Painted slate gray, the game room features a kitchenette and bar area for gathering. The wine room, opposite, uses a custom wax stain in a shade of navy.

The game room is cloaked in
outdoor fabrics so no need to
worry about wet bathing suits.

The interplay between dark and light inspires us, especially when getting the mix of furnishings and fabrics just right.

The primary bedroom has a lighter palette than some of the home's darker, moodier spaces.

Sumptuous textiles are found throughout the house, including in this seating area, opposite. The light gray draperies and pale pink pillows provide an inviting hint of color.

We specified unique fluting detailing for the primary bathroom's stone accents.

For a guest bedroom, the homeowners requested color and boldness, but without bright colors. This drapery fabric offered the perfect solution.

The guest bathroom's silver-gray
grasscloth complements the
sofa and headboard fabrics in
the adjoining bedroom.

With comfortable seating in covered areas, the line between indoors and out is blurred.

An abundance of resort-style amenities makes home living cozy, soothing, and luxurious.

The home's entry greets guests with a warm welcome and symmetry. The circular shape in the door echoes the shapes in the tile work.

GREAT EXPECTATIONS

One of the most intimidating aspects of interior design for the novice and pro alike is the concept of scale. Of course, floor plans and furniture layouts reveal a lot of information and are valuable guideposts for creating a room's design. But you also have to be able to visualize pieces in the spaces themselves, such as the vast living room of this client's residence, which features twenty-two-foot-tall ceilings. This type of space can be daunting to decorate, but our firm has devised several unique solutions over the years to help ground voluminous spaces such as this. Thankfully, this room is graced with bountiful natural light, and the delicate yet dramatic shadows it creates proved to be a unique opportunity for interplay with the furnishings as the sun shifts throughout the day.

At one end of the room, a custom screen clad in a beautiful gray-blue velvet anchors the space. It required herculean effort by our craftsmen, electricians, and contractor to design and install the piece, yet it's almost impossible to imagine anything else in its place. Behind and flanking it, beautiful floor-to-ceiling draperies add softness and lend an extra layer of dimension and visual interest to the room. This composition, as a whole, gives a sense of warmth and intimacy. Without these layers and various textural interests, a blank wall, even with a large piece of art, easily could have overpowered the room.

The room's elegant, deeply coffered ceiling also creates visual interest on what's referred to as the "fifth wall." Ceilings can often be overlooked when designing a space, but we love to celebrate them with interior architecture—such as this coffered ceiling, wall coverings, high-gloss lacquer, or other decorative finishes. The sky's the limit when it comes to options, but we prefer to keep things on the simpler side, avoiding recessed lighting whenever possible. Graceful chandeliers or classic pendant lights keep a room aglow with a warm ambiance, rather than downlights, which can be too bright and harsh. Interior design is as much about setting a mood as it is about the furnishings that occupy a space, and great lighting is key to any successful space.

The warmth and intimacy that define the living room ebb and flow throughout the entire house. There are bright and airy spaces, as well as spaces with darker, moodier colors, and colorful accents, such as citron throw pillows. Part of the inspiration for the color palette and vibe of the home came from the husband's and wife's wardrobes, and we wanted to channel that in a subtle but meaningful way. We often look to our client's personal styles for inspiration; knowing that the husband could carry off a handsome blazer in a spirited color and the wife looks great in the chosen color palette let us know that we could push the envelope when devising the color scheme for this home.

A custom screen serves as an anchor to the vast living room.

Allowing for cooking, dining, and working, the open-concept floor plan is delineated by a series of archways.

*Delicate yet dramatic shadows
create a unique interplay with
the furnishings as the sun shifts
throughout the day.*

The horizontal design of the kitchen's shiplap walls is echoed by the striped pattern of the room's window treatment. Hanging the shade from the ceiling makes the room feel taller.

A cozy banquette is tucked away enough for privacy, while still allowing connections to the kitchen and other utilitarian spaces.

The butler's pantry is always at
the ready for easy entertaining.
The powder room, opposite,
features a mix of metallic
finishes—from the polished
nickel faucet and forged sconce
to a gilded mirror.

A dozen different shades of gray give shape and depth to the family room.

With a sumptuous palette and plush textiles, the husband's study is a rich cocoon.

A bookcase in the study reveals a hidden storage area.

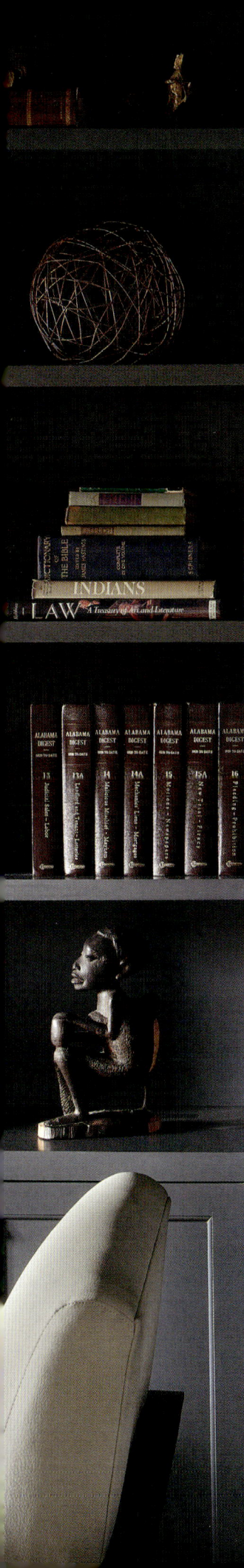

The home's primary bedroom and bath, opposite, offer an ideal place for respite.

A guest bedroom is a veritable sea of tranquility
with a hushed palette and luxurious textiles.

COLORS *of*
SAND *and* SKY

In the South, where most of our design firm's work is located, there is a beloved vacation spot that's unofficially referred to as "30A." Not only is it the name of the highway that stretches across the Florida panhandle, it is also shorthand referring to a number of Gulf Coast beach communities in the region that are connected by this stretch of road. Alys Beach is one of those special towns, and this is where the clients' second home is located. The community is known for its fresh take on Bermudan architecture, and many of the houses, such as this one, feature interior courtyards with pools or other water features. Once you enter those courtyards and hear the sound of the water trickling or splashing, you immediately feel transported, both mentally and physically.

In fact, there's a feeling of serenity in the air that blankets the entire town, and that sensibility was one of our guiding principles in creating the design of this home. A newly constructed vacation residence for a couple, their two grown children (who visit often), and a child in high school, this space needed to meet the demands of all ages. One of the things that makes this house special is its location on a corner lot, a feature unusual in the area. Because of this position, sunlight fills the house from several different directions throughout the day.

Particularly at their vacation homes, clients want to feel connected to the outdoors and often crave a light, bright palette. Nothing says "aah" like an airy palette that evokes the colors of sand at the beach, the blue of the ocean and sky above, and the tones of driftwood washed ashore. We incorporated a similarly soft palette throughout this home, with the occasional accent, such as a pale blush color in one of the bedrooms. Nothing is too high contrast or jarring, but the subtle addition of color is an unexpected delight to the eye. We love using neutral palettes but work diligently to ensure that there is always a moment of surprise or an unexpected juxtaposition, so the colors never become monotonous.

Whether it is at a primary residence or vacation property, maximizing a home's views from the indoors is essential. By the same token, we stay mindful of how to temper the sunlight, whether that's through the use of gauzy panels that billow in the wind or simple linen or wool drapery, all of which are used in this home to control the light and provide privacy at night. Even at the beach, sometimes a break from the sun is welcome.

This home, like many at Alys Beach, features deep covered loggias that we furnished with the same attention to detail given to the interior rooms, including oversized upholstered seating that encourages guests to linger longer. These outdoor dining and lounge spaces greatly expand the home's overall living space and can be used throughout the year. In fact, when it's time to entertain, the doors slide open, disappearing into the walls, and the line between indoors and out is almost completely blurred, allowing guests to move effortlessly from one space to the other.

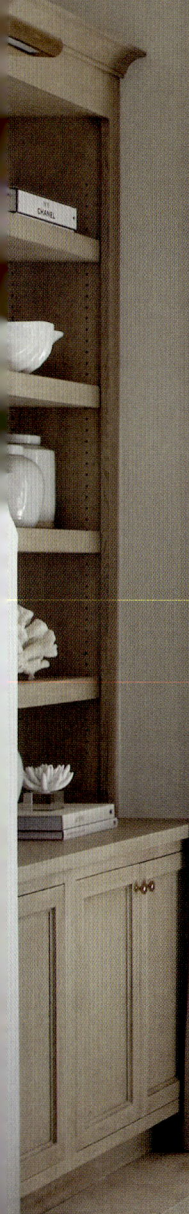

The floor-to-ceiling draperies serve two purposes: to soften the expanse of the large room and to control the sunlight, lending an ethereal quality to the space. In fact, the repetition of the curtain folds adds to the architecture of the room.

The living room features a design technique we love to implement: mixing period pieces, eras, and decorative styles to create something entirely new.

The house has no shortage of gathering spaces, including this lounge area. A bar area, opposite, conceals refrigerator drawers for drinks and entertaining essentials.

*There's a feeling of serenity in the air
that blankets the entire town, and that
sensibility was one of our guiding principles
in creating the design of this home.*

Decorative vignettes with favorite
artwork and curated collections
add a personal touch to any home.

Quartersawn white oak in a light finish gives a nod to the home's coastal location.

Our team designed much of the kitchen detailing, including the range hood and cabinet doors and drawers that feature a fluted design.

We commissioned an artist to design an installation of ceramics, opposite, for this stairwell. Plaster walls let the beauty of the architecture shine.

A chaise in the primary bedroom offers an ideal place to relax. Nailhead accents on a leather-clad console add extra detailing in an understated way. A concealed television rises from its top.

When one must work at the beach, the primary
bedroom has the perfect spot.

When the house is full of family
and friends, the primary bedroom
is an oasis of calm.

The primary bathroom's floor-to-ceiling tile installations are works of art unto themselves.

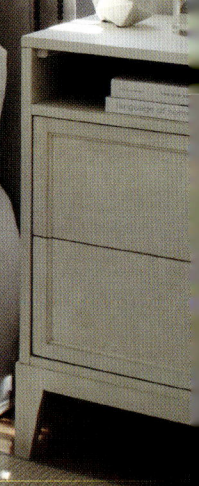

The daughter's bedroom is accented with pale blush tones. We treated the draperies to simple grosgrain trims at the top of the panels, reminiscent of a crown molding.

A pair of woven headboards
add an organic feeling to a boy's
bedroom. Iron stools provide a
sculptural touch.

The ART of the FISHING FLY

SURF TRIBE
INDIA HICKS

A WELCOMING ELEGANCE Suzanne Rheinstein

The myriad courtyards and balconies at this coastal residence often blur the line between indoor and outdoor living.

Outdoor living spaces feature furnishings and textiles as fine and detailed (and comfortable) as their interior counterparts.

The home's exterior reflects the globally
influenced architectural vernaculars found within
the community.

PRETTY *and* PRACTICAL

It probably goes without saying, but trust is one of the most important aspects of the work we do. Thankfully, we are blessed with clients who trust us, trust the process, and trust our vision. It allows us to do our very best work. In the case of this project, the clients are both highly accomplished individuals and have two active young sons. They truly entrusted us with the design of their first real family home—they reached out to us because they wanted to be intentional in its design and decoration with every decision, from the biggest to the smallest.

Many of our projects involve a high degree of interior architecture—bookcases, paneled walls, coffered ceilings, and so on—before any decorating can begin. However, in this case, the clients had an existing residence with great bones, which allowed us to focus primarily on the furnishings and to finesse finishing details. To get acquainted, we inquired into our clients' lifestyles and daily routines. This helps create spaces that are both pretty and practical. In a room that was previously a pass-through area, we added a sofa that is now ideal for sitting to put on shoes before leaving the house (or after returning home). A graphic wall covering envelops the room, making any time spent in the space feel all the more special.

In another room, a console has a drawer dedicated exclusively to storing the dog's leash, and we even added a little bowl atop the counter into which the clients can drop their keys. These might seem like minor details, but understanding the more minute habits of the homeowners' active lifestyles lets us focus on elevating the adventures of everyday life while giving them less mundane things to worry about. They are able to navigate hectic mornings or moments meant for relaxation after work and school without sacrificing style.

The spaces throughout the home have a quiet, even ethereal quality to them. Gauzy draperies create a cocoon-like effect in both the dining and living areas, although they appear as light as air and refract the sunlight in the most beautiful way. Brass and gold metal accents add a level of elegance without overpowering, and a pair of mirrors in the dining room seem to float off the walls, creating a unique three-dimensional effect.

An original bar area, backed by a wall crafted of antiqued mirror, adds a sense of time and patina to the space. We also inherited an indulgent library with navy lacquered walls, which offers a place where one can curl up and read at any time of the day; it's the perfect juxtaposition to the home's abundance of neutral tones. By letting us focus on the details, these clients have allowed us to help create a home that has filled their lives with more beauty and ease.

A sculptural chaise provides the ultimate place for rest and relaxation.

HISTORIC HOUSES OF PARIS
CARTIER DESIGN: A LIVING LEGACY
INTERIOR LOUISE BRADLEY
A Year with C. S. Lewis
STEVEN VOLPE
ROOMS
ISABELLE STANISLAS
KOICHI TAKADA
CONTEMPORARY WABI-SABI STYLE
BILLY COTTON
ROME

We enveloped the room with a blanket of sheer drapery, bringing consistency to a space with unusual window placement.

The graphic wallpaper we selected highlights
the existing wood accents, which add a sense of
architectural integrity to the room.

A dynamic midnight blue carries through the library's paint color, upholstery fabric, and animal-print rug.

The spaces throughout the home have a quiet, even ethereal quality to them.

A reflective antiqued mirror backdrop lures guests to the existing built-in bar area, with bistro-style glass-and-brass shelving and large-scale hardware to balance the heft of the cabinet.

No detail was overlooked:
natural textures offer an organic
feeling, and a formal damask
pattern, opposite, is more casual
when printed on a woven linen.

FRESH PERSPECTIVE

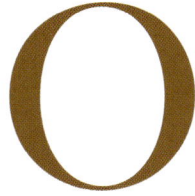

O ften when clients purchase an existing residence, the interiors can be dated or just not flow well from one room to the next. Even the floor plans of houses built just ten or twenty years ago aren't always suited for today's lifestyles. In these cases, sometimes a major renovation is in order; at other times, smaller tweaks are all that's required and even small adjustments can make a world of difference. At this beachside vacation home in Florida, we shifted the flow of space by closing off odd passageways and opening up new walls and doors. Not only did this change the flow of the home, but it shifted the general feeling of it too.

What had been a series of separate living and dining spaces that felt cramped opened up to be airy and inviting. The kitchen, for instance, had been an awkward space and not highly functional. Incorporating the adjacent hallway not only made the space larger, but also exposed it to an abundant source of natural light from a series of windows in the former passage space. Aesthetically, the house also felt a little tired, so we wanted to make it feel more beach appropriate in subtle ways. In the living room, for example, the ceiling features a series of beams that add great architectural interest. But they were stained a dark color and felt imposing. With a fresh coat of white paint, they now seem to float.

The entire living room was designed for gathering together. We wanted the space to feel upleveled, but not too precious. To keep it versatile, we incorporated a mix of indoor and outdoor fabrics, so that if someone comes in from the beach with a wet towel or damp swimsuit, nothing is going to get damaged. The textiles used exclusively in the lower-level family room are soft, and you would never guess they were designed especially for high-performance areas.

The home's private spaces have a certain carefree spirit as well, and when the house swells with visitors, the bunk room can accommodate up to six guests. Conversely, when someone is home alone, the rooms feel as cozy and welcoming for one as they do for twenty.

A bar area includes a painting evocative of the home's surrounding landscape.

The living room's paneled upholstered wall, opposite, employs a handsome picture-rail system.

We moved walls and closed up doors to create better efficiency in this coastal kitchen. The veining in the marble slab backsplashes adds visual interest.

Our team loves to focus on cabinet detailing. If the architectural detailing is great, you need less decoration.

The cozy banquette can accommodate a couple or a crowd. The table finish accentuates that of the kitchen cabinetry.

A quaint nook in the primary bedroom offers an intimate area for writing and reading. The campaign-style desk and dramatic contemporary art are alluring touches that anchor the space.

Furniture in the lounge area is covered in performance fabrics that are impervious to damp towels or swimsuits.

Throughout the home, an ethereal palette is both inviting and soothing.

Marble is a go-to in many of
our bath projects, including this
primary bath.

When we don't use marble,
decorative wallcoverings, opposite,
provide similar movement.

This home has no shortage of sleeping areas, including these special bunk beds we designed.

Alys Beach, Florida, is known for its Bermudan and Moorish architectural accents; this home features both.

EASY ELEGANCE

On paper, the clients' house prior to this project would have appeared to accommodate their family of five with ease. The square footage was ample and the number of bedrooms and baths was just right. But on the ground floor, something was amiss. The original floor plan featured not only an open concept, but also an array of boxy hallways that were not conducive to seamless flow—they consumed valuable space that wasn't being utilized to its fullest potential.

Our firm was originally called upon to problem solve by sourcing a few furniture pieces and accessories, but we quickly realized that what would get this family what they really needed from the house required structural changes. So, in collaboration with a talented architect, we began to reconfigure the existing space into areas that were much more functional and inviting. We replaced the arches—some with limestone surrounds—that segued from one room to the next with simple passages that allowed the flow between rooms to feel effortless. In the kitchen, the architect specified beautiful details, including fluting on the cabinetry and a remarkable coffered ceiling that added height and depth to the room. He was also able to annex one of the many awkward hallways into a new butler's pantry.

Most importantly, perhaps, was the family's need for comfortable, welcoming seating. As a family of five with a steady stream of visiting extended family, friends, and other guests, the clients wanted—and needed—as many different places to gather as we could possibly conceive. By reconfiguring the living room walls and removing three archways, the room became much more spacious, welcoming, and adaptable, accommodating a variety of seating options and accessories. This opened up the space remarkably well from the few pieces of furniture and limited number of people it was able to accommodate beforehand.

We love combining a mix of lighter and darker environments under one roof, and that was the strategy incorporated here. The sun-filled dining room features a beautiful, hand-painted grass cloth that we commissioned especially for this space; the husband's cozy nearby study adds mood and contrast. Those juxtapositions give the house a unique energy that amplifies what could otherwise feel like more static spaces.

When a home's floor plan doesn't quite work, many people immediately think that adding an extension is the only solution to making it more livable. What is so interesting about this house is that we did not expand its footprint. Rather, with clever solutions, the house is now living up to its maximum potential and makes the most of every existing inch with style.

This dining room is family-focused, featuring resilient fabrics, a flexible layout, and decor that balances beauty with daily functionality.

We incorporated refined
luxury along with practicality
in this space, featuring unique
storage, a neutral palette, and
inviting arrangements ideal for
gatherings.

The living room exudes quiet glamour, with unique sculptural pieces, flowing draperies, and textures that subliminally encourage tactile interaction and, in turn, a sense of calm.

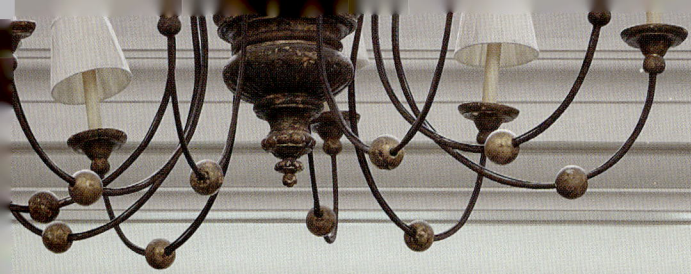

This kitchen radiates bespoke, livable elegance. A balanced layout, curated furnishings, and a serene interplay of textures and tones define the space.

We always strive to craft rooms like this kitchen that are rooted in comfort and beauty. Elegant, natural finishes and detailing create homes full of warmth, depth, and light.

We love combining a mix of lighter and darker environments under one roof.

Luxurious leather-upholstered cabinetry doors grace the bar area.

This bedroom has an airy layout, textured layers, and unique details—such as lighting and artworks—that elevate everyday living into a serene, harmonious experience.

PROJECT CREDITS

INTERPLAY *of* **LIGHT** *and* **DARK**

Photographer | John Bessler

Stylist | Eleanor Roper

Architect | Chris Tippett of Tippett Sease and Baker

Builder | Francis Bryant

HISTORIC CHARM *in a* **NEW HOME**

Photographer | Mali Azuma

Stylist | Anita Sarsidi

Architect | Frank Nola of Nola/Van Peursem Architects

Builder | William Lemaster of Lemaster Construction

COMFORT AWAY *from* **HOME**

Photographer | John Bessler

Stylist | Eleanor Roper

GREAT EXPECTATIONS

Photographer | Alison Gootee

Stylist | Anita Sarsidi

Builder | Slate Barganier

COLORS *of* **SAND** *and* **SKY**

Photographers | Max Kimbee & Alison Gootee

Stylist | Anita Sarsidi

Architect | Ron Domin of Domin Bock Architects

Builder | Gulfview Construction

PRETTY *and* **PRACTICAL**

Photographer | Alison Gootee

Stylist | Anita Sarsidi

FRESH PERSPECTIVE

Photographer | Alison Gootee

Stylist | Anita Sarsidi

Builder | Gulfview Construction

EASY ELEGANCE

Photographer | Alison Gootee

Stylist | Anita Sarsidi

Renovation Architect | Jason Robb

ACKNOWLEDGMENTS

THREE YEARS AGO, I was diagnosed with stage 4 non-Hodgkin lymphoma and began one of the most difficult journeys of my life. The plan of care began the night of my diagnosis, as I was in excruciating pain from a tumor on my spine, and they were concerned about permanent nerve damage. Treatment and complications afterward put me in the hospital several times, including one night when I was admitted with neutropenia from the chemotherapy. As my husband and I sat in that hospital room and looked out the window to the city lights of downtown Birmingham, Alabama, we wondered how life had turned upside down so quickly and if it would ever feel normal again.

I share this because if you are going through a tough time, I want you to know that light is on the other side. Light finds a way back into your life, as it did for me.

In fact, you can imagine how grateful I am to now be in this moment, giving thanks to the many people who have not only helped make this book a reality but who have also brought light into my life along the way.

I am grateful to my amazing clients who place their trust in us; my colleagues, family, and friends who helped and encouraged my career over the years; the architects, craftsmen, artisans, staff, and builders who collaborated to create amazing designs; and the talented team who brought this book to life. It is because of my friend and publicist Jenny Bradley Pfeffer that this book became a reality. She encouraged me to present my work and helped me embark on this endeavor.

Many thanks to Gibbs Smith for seeing value in sharing my work with you. I am particularly grateful to Madge Baird for her expertise and discerning eye and to Jennifer Adams for corralling all of us together to take this book to the finish line.

How could I even think of writing a book without the creative direction and expertise of Dyad principal Tom Maciag and his team? Tom encouraged me to step out of my comfort zone and let the contrast of light and dark found in my work (and throughout the book) foreshadow my life over the past few years. Thank you, Tom, for pushing me to be a little uncomfortable.

Clint Smith's talent with a pen is magical, and he did a wonderful job taking my thoughts and putting them into words. He held my hand throughout this process and provided friendship along the way.

Our projects take multiple, talented people, and I am grateful to the former and present team members who have helped our client projects come to life. I want, in particular, to thank Kimberly Powell, Eva Crawford, Mary Baylee Thomson, Ellie Wolter, Madeline Ryczek, Claire Owens, Rebecca Alpert, Monica Stewart, Abbey Dunn, Alex Woodcock, Allie Burns, and Emma Green. I am also grateful to my contemporaries, Sumner Starling and Anne Hurley, for stepping in at times to help steer the ship when I needed to focus on my health.

I find myself so very grateful for the amazing clients who have hired Dana Wolter Interiors over the past twenty years. Many have become repeat clients and now friends. Thank you for trusting us with your homes: I am honored.

I would be remiss not to mention my parents, Lucy and Jack Kubiszyn, who taught my four siblings and me the importance of family and making memories with those you love. I attribute to them my knack for finding function in any room and serenity amidst chaos.

First Edition
29 28 27 26 25   5 4 3 2 1

Published by
Gibbs Smith
570 N. Sportsplex Drive
Kaysville, Utah 84037

1.800.835.4993 orders
www.gibbs-smith.com

Designed by Dyad
Printed and bound in China

Library of Congress Control Number: 2024951605
ISBN: 978-1-4236-6728-5

This product is made of FSC®-certified and other controlled material.

FSC
www.fsc.org

MIX
Paper | Supporting
responsible forestry
FSC® C208677